Book Description

"Once in your life, try something. Work hard at something. Try to change. Nothing bad can happen!" - Jack Ma, Founder and Former Executive Chairman of Alibaba Group

Have you ever thought of how great it would feel to have enough wealth to retire early and enjoy life to the fullest? Is that thought followed by an immediate sense of gloom, knowing that it is nothing more than a pipe dream? Have you ever come across a point in life where you truly felt you had something going, but never knew how to make it big? Rest assured, you are not alone.

Every day, thousands of people wake up to the thought that today will be the day they will redefine their lives. As motivating a thought as that is, it is a shame that a large number of people end the day with a sad realization that it is impossible to achieve. Some, who do cling on to the hope of doing something big, are then bogged down by opinions from others and give up the chase. Only a soul or two actually have the nerve to hold it together and truly do something remarkable. Believe it or not, these souls are either living a luxurious life now, somewhere in the beautiful coastal islands, or they are half-way through their struggles and can almost taste the rich life they have always dreamed of.

Contrary to popular belief, retiring early is an option for most; they just don't have much faith in it. For such professionals and businessmen, things can change if they are willing to change a few things first. All they need is a source of guidance, a spark to ignite the passion and constant motivation to keep them going towards their ultimate goal.

Live In Holiday is a book that breaks all the clichés and aims to bring forth tried and tested facts, knowledge and real-life scenarios for the readers. Focusing on life's regular problems, which are often the greatest contributor behind the stagnant lives we live, the book will provide a perfect guide to kick-start your journey to a truly rich life.

Learn how to avoid the obvious issues, gain the confidence to be yourself and pursue your dreams. Develop a thorough understanding of what needs to be done in order to finally lead a life the way it is supposed to be lived.

The book will discuss various aspects such as:

- Identifying misleading information
- Re-focusing your goals and priorities
- Learning from success stories

- Identifying common reasons behind failures
- The value of time
- Effective planning
- And much more!

Live In Holiday: Live A Truly Rich Life is based on thorough research, which is why it aims to provide only the most authentic facts and figures, straight from the finest examples and sources, where possible. The book contains various ideas, notions and suggestions, each of which can be successful with proper commitment and expertise.

Retiring early to settle down happily is more than just a vision or a theory; it is a way of life. Fortunately, you have already taken your first step; why wait any longer? Grab your copy and discover just how you can start your journey to pursue the life you truly desire.

Live in Holiday

Live A Truly Rich Life

Leo Anthony Cikky

© **Copyright 2020 - All rights reserved.**

The content contained within this book may not be reproduced, duplicated or transmitted without direct written permission from the author or the publisher.

Under no circumstances will any blame or legal responsibility be held against the publisher, or author, for any damages, reparation, or monetary loss due to the information contained within this book, either directly or indirectly.

Legal Notice:

This book is copyright protected. It is only for personal use. You cannot amend, distribute, sell, use, quote or paraphrase any part, or the content within this book, without the consent of the author or publisher.

Disclaimer Notice:

Please note the information contained within this

document is for educational and entertainment purposes only. All effort has been executed to present accurate, up to date, reliable, complete information. No warranties of any kind are declared or implied. Readers acknowledge that the author is not engaged in the rendering of legal, financial, medical or professional advice. The content within this book has been derived from various sources. Please consult a licensed professional before attempting any techniques outlined in this book.

By reading this document, the reader agrees that under no circumstances is the author responsible for any losses, direct or indirect, that are incurred as a result of the use of the information contained within this document, including, but not limited to, errors, omissions, or inaccuracies.

Table of Contents

.Book Description

Introduction

Doing the Impossible
    About The Author

Chapter 1: Retiring Early - Is It Possible?
The History Behind The FIRE Concept
Never-Ending Pursuit of Happiness
    Jack Ma
    Walt Disney

Chapter 2: Those Forgotten By History
Most Common Reasons Behind Failures
    Not Knowing Your Goals
    Setting Unrealistic Expectations
    Societal Pressure
    Lacking Confidence
    Other Reason Leading To Failure
    Lessons To Learn

Chapter 3: Knowing What Defines 'Rich' For You
    Money Is What I Want
    I Want To Be Wealthy
The Biggest Luxury In Life: Time
    What To Do To Become 'Time-Rich'?
    Learn How To Spend Your Time
    Setting Your Priorities
    Use Planners
    Avoid Multitasking
    Stay Healthy
    Stay Organized

Chapter 4: Freedom - A Must Have For All
  Learn How To Say No
  Have Your Say
  Stop Fearing The Unknown
  Freedom From Work
    Some Good Investment Ideas
    Procrastination Is Not Freedom

Chapter 5: The Long Journey To Freedom
  Making A Commitment
    Plan To Win
    Learn To Remain Calm
    Stop Fearing The Worst
    Change Your Social Circle
    No More Waiting
    Stop The Negativity
  Focusing On Yourself
    Start Seeking Knowledge
    Start Focusing On Your Health
    Personal Grooming
    Needs Over Desires

Chapter 6: Creating Your Own Future
  Avoiding The Obvious Traps
    Not Seeking Help
    Settling For Less
    Keep Your Goals In Sight
    Never Give Up
  Knowing When You Are There
    Do What You Have Always Wanted to Do
    Reflect Back on Your Journey
    Lead By Example
    Continue to Invest Wisely
    Your Ultimate Reward

Conclusion

References

Introduction

"Only I can change my life. No one can do it for me." - Carol Burnett

How many times have you found yourself dreaming about the day when you would have enough money to let go of your job, buy your dream house, have a sustainable business venture and the time to do whatever you please? Quite often, I suppose. There is nothing to be ashamed about, every one of us has been through such a phase.

Any working professional of today's world can relate to the above. If we are being honest, we have often found ourselves in certain phases where everything feels like it is falling apart. Regardless of how hard we try, nothing seems to be working. This leads us to make some decisions which would hopefully change the way things are for us. Unfortunately, most of us do not think things through and immediately decide to either switch our job to one that pays better or hire someone to help us with our business. While both seem logical, they are far from being long-term solutions.

Admittedly, the wages you may be working on probably are barely able to cover all your living expenses, which isn't what you may have imagined. With almost no savings, you cannot travel once a year to get the break you richly deserve, nor save up a chunk of money to spend on your big day. It will probably take a whole lifetime for your current saving to hit that magical six figures. Keep in mind that this does not take into account the inflation rate. That, then, is a gloomy prospect. Perhaps switching your job to one that pays higher fits the bill?

A higher salary can certainly allow you to spend or save more than usual, yes, but what is the point if you will eventually be spending all that hard-earned money on flashy cars, completely unnecessary fashion accessories and then be upset about the depleting sums?

Doing a work you don't like brings stress, and prolonged stress brings ailments. Some of these ailments are life-threatening while others may push you into a suicidal zone. Either way, things aren't looking promising. It is a given that to retire early, you still do need to go through some hard work in life, but the question is how? How is that any different from the regular, routine life we are already leading?

In the second instance, by hiring someone to take care of our business or do the hard work for us, we are creating a habit of having someone around to carry out our tasks and routine activities while we lie on the couch and watch our favorite Netflix series. This is neither healthy nor a way forward. This way, the so-called solution would be short-term and would create you more issues than it solves. As for the person who is doing all the chores for you, they stand a better chance to actually do something good for their own sake.

In order to do something about our lives, we need to be the one to do things on our own. Relying on someone else or trying to search for get-rich-quick schemes will always end up in disappointment. Then what can a working professional do to be in a position to have all the money they need and be able to retire early as well?

Live In Holiday: Live A Truly Rich Life is more than just a book; it aims to serve as a map for any working professional, especially those who may have just started their professional careers. With rich information, we will walk through all the important phases on this journey and learn of the ways which have already been adopted by those who lead by example today.

Doing the Impossible

To you, the glass may be half empty, to me, it might be half full. It is only a matter of how we perceive things that separates us from those who are successful or those who are anything but successful. While we will explore numerous reasons behind failure further on within the book, I would like to point out one matter of utmost importance, and to do that, here's a little question for you to ponder: *What would be your first thought if someone walked up to you and told you that you can retire early and truly lead a rich life?*

Most would just laugh it off and immediately assume the worst. Somewhere between, "That's just impossible" and, "Here we go again" perhaps. If you came up with an answer resembling that, shrouded with doubts and questions, I assure that most of it is not your fault. It is the society that we live in which constantly feeds us the idea that such nonsense would lead to dire consequences. That then takes away any hope of pursuing the seemingly impossible.

With that said, however, here is another question to spark a bit of curiosity in you: *What if it actually works out and a few years from now, you can truly be where you want to be?*

Interesting, right? Well, the good news is that you do not need to be a rocket scientist to do that or crack some special code. Yes, it takes time but it is not as hard as many might think, as we shall find out within this book.

About The Author

Finally, it is time to address some questions. Who am I and what makes my word better and more trustworthy than of those who sell lies? If you haven't asked such a question, I am assuming you never had to deal with someone who devoured a chunk of your money and provided you with no return at all (let's hope you continue to steer clear of that).

My name is Leo Anthony Cikky. Born in the year 1988, I am someone who is comfortably seated right between Millennials and the old-timers. For being a person who has experienced both sides, in terms of technology and cultural changes, it was perhaps an obvious choice to write and allow my readers to bridge the gap between the two generations a little easier.

I love writing, and I am a passionate author. I have my academic roots dug deep within social and geopolitical studies. I graduated cum laude from the Italian University of Lecce in 2015. Ironically, even before I ever became a graduate, I had an eye out for technology. This love of mine led me to work various jobs in the field of information and communication with big names in Milan. Sure, it seemed wonderful but things just did not seem right for me.

For starters, I was living within a society that was more interested in the amount of money I made than my happiness. Add to that the fact their narrow approach to life and the instantaneous opinions they would have over matters like 'being financially free' or 'retiring early' made matters far worse.

I knew that I had to do something for myself and set myself free. Free from the age-old traditions of working 9-5 jobs, repeating the same pattern of "work, eat, sleep, repeat" and truly live life itself. Sure enough, my vision of such a life was met with harsh words, frowns and quite hard opinions. Fortunately, I decided to ignore that as I genuinely believed I was onto something. I am happy to report, things have been going rather well.

Sure, I had to make some sacrifices in the start, and I had to change the way I was living, eating and thinking. However, that was a small price to pay for the massive benefits I now get to enjoy and foresee for the coming years. This newly found passion also drove me to research quite a lot and learn from some of the finest mentors I could find.

"If you want to win in the 21st century, you have to empower others, making sure other people are better than you are. Then you will be successful." - Jack Ma

Possibly, for the very same reason, I recently decided to stop keeping this knowledge that has helped me transform my life into this exceptional time to myself and share it with those who are willing to make a change. Using my personal experience, let this book, with its rich resources and facts, guide you to pursue your truly rich life.

From here on out, promise yourself that you will believe in yourself and that you will do all it takes to be a successful person, not just better. If you are all set, and you have made a promise, let us commence our journey and start learning about the secrets which would help us achieve the impossible.

Chapter 1: Retiring Early - Is It Possible?

If you need a one-word answer to this, it is a solid yes. For generations, people have sought ways to make their lives easier. Not only that, people have gone to great lengths to find ways to further enhance their lifestyles, make things easier for themselves and allow them to live life fully. Sure enough, there have been many cases, however, we only know of a few.

Retiring early is far more than just a figment of the imagination, an idea, or a concept. It is a way of life that runs parallel to the one we are accustomed to. The only issue here is that most of us are only looking at one side of the picture. Unfortunately, the side we are looking at is the darker one.

There is no denying the fact that something continued to bother you and led you to start searching for ways to change all that and do something significant instead so that you can have a secure retirement, and an early one at that. No one likes to work for a non-desired job, and no one likes being bossed around every now and then. I know because I have been through the same as well. With that said, however, things do not need to be as tough as we are told.

With the world advancing at such an incredible pace, more and more venues of opportunities are opening up, yet we are still limiting ourselves to seeking a 9-5 job that pays moderately well. Add to that the fact that we continue to thrive on making things more complicated than they already are. How? Let us have a look at a typical scenario to understand things better.

Mr. Smith, an assistant manager, earns what others would call a handsome salary. He lives in a fancy area and is driving the latest car of his favorite make. Sounds all good, right? Of course, who wouldn't want to be in his shoes and lead such a life? However, things aren't always what they seem. Let us look at things through the eyes of Mr. Smith now and see if we can spot some differences.

Every month, Mr. Smith draws half of his salary right away, to pay the enormous rent. He then takes care of all the expenses such as utility bills, phone and internet payments, fuel expenses, grocery shopping, etc. The rest of the month, he knows he cannot dine out more than once, nor participate with friends at major league games. He is only bound to stay at home, eat whatever he cooks, watch whatever is on the television and that is it. Having another person over would push his expenses further and hence exceed his monthly income. A very tight situation that he gets to deal with every single day. All that money, and he is still not able to save any for rainy days.

In such a case, the living certainly seems attractive but the deeper you look, the more issues you discover. There are ways Mr. Smith can change all that and start saving significantly higher, but saving alone is not the aim of this book. I am not here to give you financial advice. If that was the case, I would have named this book *How To Save Money* and focused completely on that. The point here is that Mr. Smith is living in his present, with almost no planning for the future. He is taking things as he goes along, which is fine but the day he retires, he would have pretty much nothing to support him in that leg of the journey.

Retiring at the age of 60 is common; everyone does that. By this age, you cannot enjoy life fully as you are already riddled with ailments, a depreciating body and physique and all that money, even if you managed to save, would most likely be used to cover your medical bills. If I was in such a boat, I know I wouldn't be looking forward to that. So what can we do?

Believe it or not, many have already given this a thought and some serious studies were conducted.

Retiring early is no new concept. It has been pondered upon, discussed and argued over for over 300 years. However, this was only limited to the elite classes or those who had enough money to establish their own businesses. It did not start picking up pace until only recently, and that is where the rest of the world joined in this pursuit. One of the most popular movements that came, and still exists, is called FIRE.

The History Behind The FIRE Concept

Financial **I**ndependence, **R**etire **E**arly (FIRE) - A model introduced in 1992, quickly became a hit with the Millennials and has attracted a global audience. The model is designed to aim for financial independence and early retirement. The idea behind FIRE is simple; gather assets to the point that the resulting passive income covers all living expenses in perpetuity. That is not all as there are other components which one must ensure in order to fully be able to retire early.

The FIRE concept follows a strict routine where one is forced to cut out all expenses to a bare minimum, thus allowing a jaw-dropping savings of 70%. That means, Mr. Smith would have to move from his apartment to a single room, somewhere further away from the posh area. It also means that he would have to get rid of his car and settle for travelling by bus, subway or other modes of public transportation. Mr. Smith would also be required to let go of quite a lot of things and stick to his necessities alone. Such a strict routine would net him a handsome savings by the end of the year.

As per the FIRE plan, one can retire as early as 40 or 50, depending on when you start following FIRE and when you feel like you have made enough money.

Behind every early retirement plan, there are three things that play an important role.

1- Longevity - The number of years you will live. The first factor alone is a bit of a challenge. No one can guess how long they will have to live before they pass away. This point is basically to remind ourselves how many years, on average, do we think we will have and then use that information to start crunching numbers. After all, you need to know how much money you need in order to cover your expenses after your retirement.

2- Costs - This is the cost of the life that you dream to live each year. Maybe you are someone who would love to live in Monte Carlo. Perhaps you are someone who would prefer the countryside. Each would have varying costs. The more accurate your studies or estimates, the better the results. You may wish to keep inflation in mind too. The more time we have to live, the more expensive life will become.

3- Savings - This is where things will sound grim. The average American is able to save around 3.5%, and that is one of the lowest numbers in history. Clearly, the average American will never be able to retire, let alone retire early. It is a crisis that needs to be averted, and for that, savings must be increased significantly.

In all of the three factors, one thing is certain: you need to work far too hard and live far too restricted in order to have a remote chance of saving enough money to retire easily, if not early. The probability isn't looking that good then.

The FIRE concept, while it garnered quite a lot of fame, managed to attract some severe criticism. For starters, it was anything beyond what any ordinary person would like to do or be willing to do. Secondly, the extremely high saving rate means that people with low income are likely to never meet their basic needs. This then gave birth to the idea that the entire FIRE concept was designed for the rich.

Frankly, the above was something that I considered for myself as well. Being someone who is young, it certainly did make sense to me. However, with a bit of research, it soon dawned on me that I was never going to be able to save enough as I had to pay my rent, my grocery bills, the utility bills and so on. The remaining sum would not even be 20% of my gross income.

Naturally then, the world started losing interest and started exploring other areas to fulfill their desires and dreams of retiring early. This paved way to a flood of ideas which, thanks to social media, started gaining reputation. While there were hundreds of thousands of opinions, suggestions and seemingly workable strategies, let us look at a few which sound quite promising, to say the least.

Never-Ending Pursuit of Happiness

The FIRE concept had just been introduced, and this clearly opened a completely new front for the rest of the world. This new trend saw many ideas, concepts and suggestions appear from all parts of the world. Almost every other person would come up with something that sounded promising but was either short-lived or unrealistic in nature. Picking out something that truly helped the case was getting more and more tricky. It was not until a book named, *Your Money or Your Life* by Vicki Robin and Joe Dominguez came onto the scene and revived the hopes of hundreds of thousands of people.

This book served as a map for many who were lost in their search for the ultimate way to achieve financial independence. While the book itself is hailed as one of the all-time greats, it did eventually start fading into the pages of history. Do not get me wrong, it was not the book that brought its decline but it was the ever-changing times and needs of the people which altered the situation. Seeing that this book originally came out in 1992, some of the ideas shared within its pages now stood obsolete or far too hard to achieve, given the constant inflation the world has faced. Surely, something else was needed to fill the void.

The first decade of 2000 saw rise to many get-rich-quick schemes. People, driven by emotion and frustration, took part in these schemes and genuinely believed they would forever change their lives. To some it actually did, but they were mostly the ones who came up with such illusions. As for those who followed these schemes, it did not fare well for them as most ended abruptly or turned out to be nothing more than a hoax.

For anyone who is not a Millennial, you may remember the 'timeshare' scheme. Timeshare, for the people who may not know, is a kind of investment where numerous people would buy a property for a fixed period of time instead of buying the entire property permanently. This allowed many to invest into buildings or units and be owners of said assets for anywhere between a week to several weeks. They would get to enjoy the benefits of being an owner and then pass the unit on to someone else. It was certainly a way to generate some passive income. The downside was that many fraudsters were also paying attention to such schemes. This then opened a floodgate for fraudulent activities and thousands were scammed into thinking they had invested into a timeshare whereas their investment would actually be usurped by scam artists via calls or emails.

Then came the era of Multi-Level Marketing. These involved a pyramid structure approach where you would be asked to 'buy' certain services or products and earn revenue for every referral you would bring in. Once you buy something from these companies, you would stand at the top of your own pyramid. In order to make money, you would need referrals under you.

For each referral you would bring, you would need another member to balance both the left and the right wings. This might not sound hard, but those who may have experienced this would know just how ridiculously difficult it became. With products that did not provide much value, it was increasingly hard to invite a referral to voluntarily pay $250 or more to sign up as a member and then invite more people just like everyone else. The only people who would make money here would be the ones at the very top. For people like us, profit was a mere dream. Eventually, many countries started to ban such activities, declaring them as illegal. Late or not, the damage was done and once again the dream of truly rich life was crushed, to say the least.

However, now, things are looking better. With the internet replacing our means of communication, verification, and information, things are far more transparent than ever before. Type in "investment ideas" and your Google search page will be riddled with millions of search results.

Now, you can do things sitting right at home and start making some serious money. From things like blogging and video logging (vlogs) all the way to freelance work, you can find something productive and rewarding throughout the internet. But, and this is a big one, most of us still do not know which ones we should pick to keep us going and help us increase our savings.

The whole idea behind retiring early hinges on the fact that we are making enough money to somehow cover our expenses and still save a chunk of money at the end of the month. With so many opportunities at hand now, you might think it is easy to pick one and stick to it. Right you maybe, but do not forget that the rest of the world has already picked up on the idea as well. The competition today is far more fierce than you might imagine.

Truly then, the most viable way you can move towards your desired retirement age is to continue working for the next decade or so. It may not be what you wish to hear, but as we go further into the book, it will make more sense. For now, just know that this is the safest bet you have in order to have a remote chance of making it to your retirement with some ease.

Disappointed? I never said this is the only way to do so. While it might be the most viable, it is not perfect, and that is exactly what we will exploit later on in this book. Our motive is to make the most out of the opportunity, and I intend to do just that. In the following chapters, I will be putting you through some thought-provoking scenarios and throwing some questions your way. Your job is to think clearly and decide how you would like to proceed.

The pursuit of happiness and early retirement is hard, but it is not impossible. By utilizing our skills, picking up new ones, or by following our passions, we just might be able to hit the bullseye well before the retirement age of 60.

The biggest hurdle that we would face, when following something we are passionate about or think is important, is the barrage of negativity that would come our way. What makes it even worse is the fact that the source of such strong negativity would be the people we love or are close to. What we must remember in such circumstances is to only take opinions from those who have actually found success through these methods. Asking a doctor how good software engineering is would end with you being demotivated by someone who has never actually experienced such a field.

The world is brimming with success stories, many of whom have gone on to make a name for themselves with the global audience. They have faced hardships most of us cannot even fathom, yet their determination and clear vision are what drove them forward. Their resilience and perseverance are what kept them going until eventually they dominated the world, quite literally.

Jack Ma

There are millionaires, there are billionaires, and then there is Jack Ma. A Chinese icon in the world of e-commerce, he is currently 55 years old and one of the richest people on Earth, with a total net worth of $44.3 billion. If you are thinking that he was perhaps the son of a wealthy father, you are greatly mistaken.

Jack Ma had a rough childhood. Born in China, he had a thing for the English language. From a very young age, he started learning the language and used it frequently. To further improve, he would eventually start giving 17-mile-long rides to foreigners on his bicycle, just so he could converse in English with the tourists. With tougher years ahead, Jack Ma only just made it through his Bachelor's degree and applied numerous times to Harvard, only to be rejected each time. Things weren't good on the job front either. He was rejected for almost every job he applied for, including one at KFC.

It was only after he was hired as a lecturer that he finally started earning something relatively good. His trip to a friend in the United States, however, is what changed everything for him.

Learning about something called the internet, he was intrigued and wanted to try it out himself. Upon searching for China, he was unable to find anything on the internet. It was this idea of bringing China on the digital map of the internet which paved the way to one of history's most successful e-commerce ventures, Alibaba.

Jack Ma quit his job and created Alibaba with a group of friends in his apartment. A project that started in 1999, it quickly went on to become China's symbol of e-commerce. Today, Alibaba is one of the biggest, if not the biggest of all, business-to-business e-commerce platforms on Earth..

The beauty behind it all is that he never gave up pursuing his dream. While the world laughed at his strange wish of bringing China on the map, and trying to prove those who rejected him for jobs wrong, he eventually became a person anyone would be honored to work for.

The strategies he used are rather evident through his quotes. He spent more time working for something he loved and ensured he only spent money on things that were essential and necessary. Being someone who is not remotely connected to programming or web development, he confessed he never wrote a single line of code. Instead, he hired someone to do the job for him, a gamble that paid off for much more than numbers could show.

- He **persevered** through thick and thin
- He **believed** in his vision
- He **worked** to the point where he knew he had found his true calling
- He **never gave up** on his dreams

The result? Jack Ma wrote history, not just for himself or China, but for the entire world to learn from.

Jack Ma officially retired from his duties at Alibaba group in September 2019, and started pursuing philanthropy. A perfect end to an illustrious career, and a perfect example for the world to follow. Not only did he make a fortune, he is now seeking what his heart desires and has all the time in the world to do just that.

Walt Disney

This may sound bizarre but the man who gave the world Mickey Mouse and many other classic characters was fired from his job at a local newspaper agency for lacking imagination. The following few years of setting a lucrative business failed miserably as well. However, his perseverance and determination saw him through. Not long after, the world welcomed *Snow White*, and the rest became history.

Walt Disney, the man that single-handedly changed the American animation industry, made it to his goals. His journey was riddled with failures, problems, a nervous breakdown, an ongoing cancer that eventually took his life, and challenges. Where the remainder of the world laughed at his ideas, he never gave his passion a second thought and today, the very same world stands in awe of what he was able to accomplish.

- Trust
- Believe
- Persevere
- Never give up

There are countless stories, and some of these you might already know. From Oprah Winfrey to Bill Gates, from J.K. Rowling to Jim Carrey, everyone started out in life in the same boat as us. What made them achieve such phenomenal success is their ability to adapt quickly, persevere and believe in what they were pursuing.

All of these had to sacrifice quite a lot, like cutting costs, quitting school and making ends meet by taking up part-time jobs. Their objective was never to retire early, but it was to seek a life they wanted to lead. By doing just that, they quickly gained the option to retire for good any given day they desire.

Finally, I would like to quote Jim Carrey to address the most important aspect of the entire "retiring early" concept. *"I wish everyone could experience being rich and famous, so that they'd see it wasn't the answer to anything."*

Yes, we need money to take care of our expenses, but it has never been the answer to everything. Changing your perspective about money and how it controls you can greatly help you achieve a lot more. With that said, here's how to proceed from here on out.

As a first step to your journey, decide that by the age of 50, you will retire come what may; not a day later than that. Keep reminding yourself that you will do whatever is necessary, and legal, to ensure you achieve that. Draw motivation from reading more about successful personalities and stories. The more you surround yourself with such motivations, the greater the impact you will feel on your personality.

Now that you have your target set, it is time for us to dive deeper into the book and rediscover some concepts, learn from the mistakes of those who suffered and failed and find our own calling as well. All of these combined will help us know exactly what we need to do. Without any of these, we are a ship in the middle of the sea, without sails or any sense of direction. We would be rocking back and forth at the mercy of the waves, and that is the definition of being lost.

Chapter 2: Those Forgotten By History

The biggest fear anyone can have is the fear of failing. Naturally, we set out to achieve our goals and by the end of the day, we either succeed in doing so or we fail. There is no middle ground, or at least we are told.

The fact is, there is always something at the end of the day for you. For all the effort that you put into something, you get a proportional result. The trouble is that for most things there is no set mechanism to determine how much of our efforts were productive and how much more we need to do in order to fully achieve a successful result.

This then introduces us to a problem. We can either continue working towards our goal relentlessly, hence sacrificing almost every hour of the day, or we can just do our jobs for the sake of it and that's that. The first situation would see us ending with issues like:

1. Stress
2. Peer pressure
3. Keeping up with the competition
4. Anxiety
5. Depression
6. Insomnia
7. Other medical and psychological issues

By the time we retire, anything we have saved would go down the drain, courtesy of the medical expenses. The result is nothing more than a failure to address the situation correctly.

The second situation would see us ending up with similar issues but the lack of motivation and energy would eventually get us laid off from the job, and unemployment alone would put a massive dent into the savings and pride of a working professional. Needless to say, that would end up in failure as well.

We as human beings are susceptible to doubts, misunderstandings and are rather quick to assume things straight away. Based on what we may have heard or seen, we immediately jump to conclusions and think "Yes, I will do exactly that!" after seeing someone flourish in a specific field. The failure here is to address the fact that things change with time. What may seem profitable today might not be profitable tomorrow.

Remember Nokia? They were once the king of the hill and then came the time of the smartphones. Even though Nokia did nothing wrong, it failed miserably and hence had to restart all over again. They were under the false assumption that their position within the market was untouchable and unsurpassable. Surely, their assumption proved fatal. A massive mistake made by such a giant is a lesson for us all to learn from. Being stubborn about something you do and trying not to adapt to changes will soon see you become obsolete, and no one in today's world values that.

Adapting to change is a major element in order to ensure our chances of success in the coming years. Failure to do so would see us forgotten within the pages of history. All that effort, all that time spent would go in vain while someone a little smarter would replace us and literally steal the spotlight from us.

In the previous chapter, we looked into the brief history of how the early retirement concept came to life and how many scams and fraudulent activities followed. We looked at the notoriously famous FIRE concept, and then we looked at the criticism the world had for it. Some of those criticisms were justified.

What I would further like to highlight here is the fact that FIRE is not the only concept that supposedly worked for many. Apart from the traditional retirement concept, where a person would work until the age of 67 years and then retire, there are some other concepts which appeared and seemed promising. While that does sound a little encouraging, I once again would like to stress that without the ability of adapting to change and changing yourself as well, none of them would remotely work for anyone.

We will also be looking into these concepts in a later chapter and compare how each had its advantages and disadvantages. There is a possible case scenario where you might just find the answer you were looking for, however, there are things which we need to understand first before taking the next step, apart from the already highlighted factor of adaptability.

In order for us to take a productive step forward, we need to explore some of the most commonly identified reasons behind failure. Why do we need to look at those? Simply to create awareness so that we do not end up making the same mistakes and end up regretting what we did. Let's face it, time is a commodity none of us can afford to lose, and no sum of money can buy you the time you lost back. The only productive and true way to move forward is to utilize time correctly. To help us with that, let us look at some of the most common reasons behind failures.

Most Common Reasons Behind Failures

Knowing is half the battle, and this cannot be truer when it comes to early retirement. If we are to truly seek out a life we desire to lead by the end of our journey, we need to know the pitfalls, the obvious traps and disastrous mistakes which can ruin our chances and force us to restart all over again. All of these are applicable to every single person, but, as mentioned above, these will have a profound impact for those seeking to chase the ultimate goal: a life without worries and full of riches.

Not Knowing Your Goals

You just finished your degree, great! You are excited by the idea of finally landing a job and earning a decent sum to allow you to lead a life of your own. You go through various job postings and start sending emails to each one of them. Before you know it, you receive a response from a firm that invites you for an interview. The process went rather well and you are eventually hired, and that is fantastic. Here is my question to you: "What happens next?"

Sure, you think you would continue working and make some money, and that would be that. Fine enough, but is that truly the goal you seek?

Now, you start questioning your own decisions as things get tougher. The salary you are drawing is barely able to meet your expenses. Your savings are not exactly growing at a steady rate. The inflation too is taking a toll on your expenses. At this rate, you figured out that you will be spending more than your actual income by the end of X number of years. Quite a frightening realization, right?

The only one to be blamed here is yourself. Harsh, but it is true. With no specific goal in mind, you continued to work, earn and spend, without ever realizing that this type of life is leading you towards more tougher times ahead. Had you started off with short-term and long-term goals, things may have been different.

This is one of the most common mistakes I have noticed throughout the world. People, working perfectly well at their job, still manage to suffer due to lack of clear goals in sight. They have the money, and the savings but have no idea about what they truly wish to do by the end of the month, year or by the time they retire.

When you come up with a solid plan, things change. If you know you are to save a certain amount of funds, for whatever reason, by the end of the year, you will take measures accordingly. You will start cutting down on your expenses and change the way of living. Small things like cooking your own meals instead of going for take-out, taking a bus to work instead of a cab, so on and so forth. These may seem small but when you crunch the numbers, the resulting amount you end up saving by the end of the month sees a significant rise. Where you were once able to save $300 a month, you might now be saving around $1000 or more. By the end of the year, you would have a good five figures within your savings, and that sounds and feels rather good.

"You cannot change your destination overnight, but you can change your direction overnight!" - Jim Rohn

All it takes is for you to ask yourself a few questions. You can use these as many times as you like, throughout various phases of your life, and it should provide you with a clear sign of the direction you are heading to and whether you are on track or otherwise.

1. What will I gain out of doing what I am doing?

2. What are my short-term and long-term goals?

3. What do I need to change about myself that is keeping me back?

4. Is there anything that I can change or get rid of which is not helping my cause?

5. Can I live without spending time and money on such things?

6. Is this really necessary?

7. How will this affect my finances?

8. How different would my life be after achieving said goals?

9. Are the goals I have for myself specific, measurable, attainable, realistic and time-bound (SMART)?

If needed, note these questions down somewhere easy to access. Answering these questions truthfully will clarify quite a lot of things. Remember, a successful goal is one that truly changes your life for the better and allows you to measure your success in one way or another, without jeopardizing your current state of living, savings or ability to perform.

Setting Unrealistic Expectations

There is a line, not a fine one, between dreaming big and setting unrealistic expectations. While being realistic is the safest way to go about your matters, sometimes we cannot help but dream big. It is because of these big dreams that most of us end up with a renewed spirit, a higher motivation and a chance to prove to ourselves that we can truly make a difference.

However, owing to the rather bleak line that divides the two, it is often easy to fall into the trap of setting unrealistic expectations for ourselves. That is quite a bit of an issue as we shall now see.

Unrealistic expectations would see a person thinking they can conquer the world, or perhaps become a billionaire overnight. These dreams are absurd and virtually impossible to achieve. If we are being honest, quite a lot of us have slept with the idea of waking up to do something so radical that it would make us a fortune within a very short span of time. We planned something, we gave it a good thought and executed everything to perfection, yet we ended up far, far away from the expected result. Why? Because we started with an expectation that was never really achievable.

Having such bizarre expectations leads to equally unrealistic goals. Here are some common examples of such goals that most of us, including myself, have either set or experienced. The result is anybody's guess.

- **- Setting goals to earn a million dollars a year -** unless you already have a major business in place that is doing absolutely well, or are employed with a six-figure salary every month, the only other way you can end up doing this is by winning some kind of a lottery or a number of jackpots in a row.

- **- Trying to lose a staggering amount of weight quickly -** We have all seen this happen. Every good thing comes with time. Losing those extra pounds requires you to undergo a tough exercise routine, a controlled diet and quite a lot of patience. Unless you are a fan of going for a surgery, it is impossible to humanely lose a massive amount of weight in a matter of a month or two.

- **- Aiming to make your business into a multi-million-dollar entity within a year -** Sure, no one stops you from dreaming big, but setting goals such as this one are just absurd. Even Alibaba, the multi-billion-dollar empire, took well over a decade to become what it is today.

Setting such overly-ambitious goals would only end up with disappointment, shattered confidence, and a bruised ego.

Societal Pressure

The only thing free in this world is an opinion. I genuinely believe that to be true. Whether we want them or not, they will always come pouring into our lives, pointing out the so-called flaws and eventually forcing us to reconsider our decisions and future goals.

I personally find this to be a major contributor to most failed cases. It is perhaps the most common problem in existence and can be seen almost everywhere, on any given day.

Suppose you decide to do something new, such as buying a new car, you are immediately met with a barrage of comments, opinions and suggestions, even if you never asked for them.

If that doesn't make you feel agitated, observe the people who come up with their opinions and suggestions. More than half of these people would have never owned such a vehicle or even be remotely well-versed with the field of automobiles. People would make up stories of how their 'friend' had the very same car and how horribly it ended for him. Some would approach you and start giving you buyer's advice, most of which would make no sense whatsoever. In the end, your decision to buy the car you wanted would be left questioning, and you would be having all kinds of doubts.

If you give up on your goal here, you would have succumbed to pressure. If you end up buying the vehicle, people would now start commenting on how they tried to help but you didn't listen. I am sorry but that is absolutely unnecessary. If you feel the car would suit you well, and your research about said car met your expectations, that is all that should matter.

Lacking Confidence

Yet another issue that many of us face. However, unlike many before, this one seems to be more relatable to us on a personal level.

All of us, male or female, young or old, have at least thought of starting our own venture once, if not more. We carried out our research and the figures look promising. The initial capital isn't exactly in hundreds of thousands of dollars, which is a further advantage.

Yes, we are tormented by the regular opinions and suggestions, most of which will continue to discourage us and our efforts. Suppose we somehow manage to look past that, we still end up giving up the idea altogether, and that has everything to do with our own confidence.

For many businessmen, it is understood that they can never succeed if they are not willing to take risks. Ask any business in existence and you will find out just how many risks it takes in order to break the barrier and make good profits in return. The problem with us, the salaried folks, is that we fear the idea of losing our only source of income for chasing something that may or may not work. The biggest enemy here is the "what if?" questions. The more we pay attention to these questions, the more we lose confidence in our brilliant plan. The minute you start doubting, you start losing your nerve.

This goes well for almost any kind of plan that you may make in life. Whether you plan on retiring early or aim to quit your job for another one, or marry someone you love, too many "what if" questions would ruin your plan. Instead of letting them control you, control them by addressing any foreseeable issue beforehand.

Since we are aiming to learn about doing something well that can allow us to lead a far better life in the future, think of all the issues that you expect to encounter, and prepare for some issues which might pop up without prior notice, such as losing a job. Know how to handle these situations and prepare your mind accordingly, and most of your worries and fears would end up fading away.

Other Reason Leading To Failure

There are some other reasons that we all must be aware of and learn how to encounter, avoid or control as they arrive. The bad news is that most of these will be inevitable. The good news, however, is that preparing for these beforehand would allow us to have all the confidence and knowledge needed to tackle them, even in the toughest of situations.

- **Lack of persistence** - Giving up far too soon when the going gets tough.

- **Lack of conviction** - Giving into demands, even though they may be morally incorrect, just to be accepted in a job, a firm or a circle.

- **Rationalization** - Blaming fate, the late bus to the office, health issues or any other excuse that one can use to rationalize failures. Instead, try analyzing your failures and learn how you could improve in the future.

- **Being ignorant of past mistakes** - You can either live or you can live and learn. Admittedly, we tend to be living our lives without reflecting back on our mistakes. We make mistakes, and that is perfectly natural. What makes it worse is the fact that we tend to repeat the same mistakes. That shows that we never really paid attention to what went wrong nor bothered to learn from our past mistakes. It's a simple trick that can change quite a lot of things for us.

Lessons To Learn

After going through all of these common errors and blunders, it is safe to say that we do have a great tendency to make mistakes. The good news is that we have an even greater capability to avoid most of these and learn from the ones we failed to avoid the first time around. The big takeaway is rather simple.

1. Stop paying attention to the unnecessary noise and opinions
2. Start trusting your instincts
3. Stop rationalizing failure with excuses
4. Know your goals and remove all ambiguities
5. Learn how to set the right expectations and SMART goals
6. Learn from your previous mistakes
7. Be consistent and determined

8. Be confident

Start working on these right away, and I assure you these will help you feel a lot better and gain quite a lot more in life, even if you intend to pursue something completely different than early retirement.

Moving forward, we will now be addressing the elephant in the room; one that has been with us since the start of this book. We will look at exactly what it means to be rich, and I guarantee, quite a lot of people may be surprised.

Chapter 3: Knowing What Defines 'Rich' For You

Nowhere in my entire life did I ever feel so lost in seeking the true definition of a single word. It is one of life's biggest mysteries, and yet we remain unphased and completely unaware of the complex nature of this word.

As a social experiment, I tried asking about 20 people whether they would like the idea of being rich. Needless to say, every single one of them said they would love to. However, my next question stumped most of them and, as a result, I ended up getting 20 different answers. The question that I asked was simple: How would you define being rich?

It is of little surprise that each one of them was stunned by my question. Frankly, if anyone was to ask me this a year or so ago, even I would have raised my eyebrow and wondered if this person had completely lost his mind. Just like in the previous chapter, where we saw how assuming things would lead to issues, we naturally tie meaning to the word 'rich' and assume there is no other meaning involved. If you want to succeed in your plan to retire early or get rich by the time you hit your retirement, you first need to understand what defines 'rich' for you.

This is a common problem we all face. We know what we want to do, but when it comes to defining things to someone or jotting them down on a piece of paper, we are absolutely lost for words. In a similar fashion, I asked a few people to define what beauty is for them. Each one of them had different ideas about what they perceived as beauty.

It is imperative for us to know exactly what we want to achieve, and that means to dive deep into the meaning that is important for us. Since we are learning about all the nitty-gritty of living a truly rich life, we need to fully understand what exactly defines 'rich' for us. As for the 'why' it is rather simple; to some, money might be what they are after, while to others, they may be seeking something else entirely.

Take a moment or two and grab a pen and paper. Sit calmly and relax. Let go of any unnecessary thought for a while and focus on answering this question.

What type of rich person do I want to be?

Think clearly and answer as concisely as possible. I know, most would end up writing things like having a lot of money, being loaded with wealth and so on. However, even that would be a start. It is a positive step forward and a bit of a self-exploration as well.

Now, put that answer aside and dive into the next sections. By the end of the chapter, I will ask you to revisit your answer. There is a possibility you might get better ideas later on and add those to your answer.

Money Is What I Want

The most obvious choice by a country mile. Everyone wants to be rich by having quite a lot of money, and for good reasons too. There are those who claim money cannot buy happiness. If you live with that perspective, you might be in for a bit of surprise.

I am not saying money can buy everything, but I sure have changed my opinion about this concept. Money can buy you happiness, and that is how the real world operates. Money can buy you:

1. A house
2. A mansion
3. Luxury cars
4. A rich lifestyle
5. The finest products in the market
6. The best health facilities
7. Exceptional comfort
8. Jewellery
9. Food

10. Clothes

11. Water and beverages

Pretty much anything that is either a necessity or a desire, money can get you that. How does it buy happiness then? The minute you end up buying something you have been saving for, imagine the sheer excitement, the sense of accomplishment and happiness that you are immediately filled with. Take away the money, and you can never even imagine that, let alone experiencing it.

There is no shame, nor should it be frowned upon, if you want to make quite a lot of money and be that type of a rich person. Regardless of what the movies show, being financially rich is a desire many of us have.

This type is specific, and that is exactly what we intend to achieve by answering the question I posed earlier. Here, the only object of interest is money, nothing more and nothing less.

I Want To Be Wealthy

"Wait a minute, isn't that the same as having a lot of money?" In a nutshell, no. Having money is focusing on one asset, and that is cash. Being wealthy is a completely different realm.

Being wealthy means that one would have quite a lot of assets such as properties, tools, vehicles, investments, clothes and money included.

"Oh, so this is the kind of rich I want to be." Precisely! Many of you may have already picked up your paper containing your answer and scratched out the previous version. However, if you haven't already done that, I suggest you wait just a little more.

Being wealthy is quite a broad phrase. Even this contains various meanings and aspects for us to cover. By aiming to be wealthy, you need to know what is wealth for you and how you intend to achieve that goal by the end of the journey. Remember, think clearly, think SMART goals and be realistic. To further help you, here are some ways to define wealth.

- **Wealth as income** - Quite self-explanatory. If you are aiming to earn a significant amount of money as a monthly/annual income, this is the type of wealth you are targeting.

- **Wealth as net worth** - Sure, we all want to be someone like the giants we keep on hearing about. With net worth in millions of dollars, the idea is very much attainable. All you need is some money to start investing, and a good eye to know when to pull your investments out for a significant margin of profit. If you intend to lead the life of an investor and be known for your wealth in terms of net worth, this is the kind of wealth you seek.

- **Wealth as a lifestyle** - There are those of us who may not find what we are looking for in the above two subtypes, perhaps this might be what you are aiming for. As per a survey by Spectrum Group, carried out in 2014, it showed that most wealthy people did not own luxury boats, mansions, nor did they spend a fortune on cars. Most spent $50,000 on a car, around $10,000 on jewelry a year and pretty much the same on fashionable accessories. The only thing they were known for is the ability to spend a significant amount on vacations (Livingston, 2020). For those seeking this flashy lifestyle, this is your definition of wealth.

- **Wealth as satisfaction** - If you are someone who is aiming for a bigger picture, someone who isn't necessarily worried about how much money you may have made, saved or invested, this might be it. You are saving all that wealth so that one day you can lead your days the way you please, without ever worrying about going to work and earning more.

I was to emphasize the last point a little more. That is what I perceive of wealth; regardless of how much I may have, as long as I can meet my needs, I do not need to worry at all. However, your case might be different.

Being rich does not necessarily mean you have all those typical assets and materialistic luxuries, sometimes you only need the satisfaction of knowing you can lead a perfect day and it will be covered by whatever wealth you may have. You use all your resources to make things easier for you so that you can have more time.

If someone is earning $50,000 a year, and this person is able to meet all his needs easily, he is already rich. Why? Simply because his definition of being rich differs from the rest of ours. He has the time he needs to enjoy subtle moments in life and cherish them. It's safe to assume the thing that is most valuable for most of us is time. Depending on the kind of life you seek, if you are making enough money, you can literally buy yourself the time to do what you want, how you want and where you want, and that is life's true luxury.

The Biggest Luxury In Life: Time

Why is it that we keep on hearing "time is luxury" over and over again? What makes time so special? Can we not worry about time at a later stage in life? These are some of the most burning questions on everyone's minds, and rightly so.

Time is indeed a commodity, one that most of us take for granted. With each passing second, we are nearing our inevitable exit from the face of the Earth. Time can be a rewarding thing or equally harsh and cruel. While there are so many things in life we can control, time is one of those elements which we can never control. Once, I asked someone why time is such an important aspect of life, and the reasons I received were more than enough to serve as an eye-opener.

- The only thing that stands between life and death is time, and unfortunately, that is decreasing every second.

- Time is eternal. Simply put, it has never stopped for anyone nor will it ever do so in future.

- It is universal. Whether you live in Japan, Mongolia, the Middle-East, or Europe, every second holds precisely the same value for everyone.

- They say opportunity never knocks twice, and that is because in the time you spent doing something else, you missed your window. That time is never coming back.

Even a flower knows when it is supposed to blossom, so how come we human beings are so unaware of time's importance? Driven by a constant search of wealth, fame and fortune, we lose track of time and end up regretting every second we wasted doing something that proved to be unproductive in the end.

After having explored the impact of lost time, let us ponder over how exactly this plays a part in our search for that truly rich life we intend to seek.

It is said that poor people waste time while the rich buy time. Impossible as it may sound, it is actually something worth considering. It is quite doable. By letting someone else do something that would waste your time, such as removing all the leaves from your garden, you buy yourself time to do something else. As an example, imagine hiring someone for $20 per hour to do the job that would take three hours. Your annual wage, when broken down, is around $50 per hour.

Now, here's the interesting bit. You buy time by hiring this person and end up paying $60. In that time, you can focus on your work for the same three hours, or perhaps pick up a project online, and you end up making $150 dollars within the same period of time. If you are already making good money, you can actually enjoy those three hours doing something you love such as watching a movie, going around the corner for a quick drink or two with your friends or even catching some sleep.

To us, we crave money and wealth. The rich, on the other hand, crave time. It is safe to say our way of thinking is poles apart. Many accounts in history show great emperors, kings and queens quoting how they wish they could exchange all the wealth and money for more time.

After reading the above, you may have actually thought you are low on time, and that you need to get things done quickly. However, time does work in a funny way. If we rush trying to achieve something that otherwise takes long, we will either end up with a completely different thing or we might end up in trouble that may have dire consequences.

Here is a simple example to further highlight the importance of time. Try and bake a cake within one minute from scratch. Unless you have some superpower that allows you to slow down time, it is humanly and mathematically impossible to do so. What you will end up with is a runny dough that is neither baked nor ready to consume. You need time for everything to fall into its place.

Similarly, chasing a dream to be rich, wealthy and successful, you need to go through the time needed to achieve that. The beauty here is that it can be done earlier by changing a few things about our lives.

"The key is in not spending time, but in investing it." - Stephen R. Covey

That is indeed the case. Time is not going to stop, that much is fully understood. To make things go our way, it is essential that we start taking time seriously and start managing it properly. We can spend the remainder of the day in leisurely activities if desired, but it is mandatory that we invest our time in productive work that either fetches us some measurable results or some kind of gain. Only then we are likely to succeed in life.

In this pursuit of ours, time plays an all-important role. Without managing time properly, all that planning, all those ideas and goals would fall apart. Everything has a place and time, and it is up to us to realize what needs to be done when.

For salaried people, you have the option of working overtime, but instead, consider a weekend job to further add to your savings. For businessmen, sacrificing leisurely activities and focusing more on productivity and lead generations may fetch you a heftier profit by the end of the month. It is hard, but it is the only way forward if you are already tight on budget.

Fear not though, as I will provide you with some great tips you can use to learn how to better manage your time and focus on things that are important.

What To Do To Become 'Time-Rich'?

If I was to highlight the central idea here, it would be easy. Time is the only true thing that matters. Without it, all your money and assets are simply worth nothing. Therefore, it is mandatory for everyone, rich or poor, to learn how to manage time properly.

The better you manage your time, the more you will be able to do in your life. There is absolutely no point in doing something throughout the day which otherwise would take just a few hours. It simply means you are not doing things right, nor prioritizing matters as they should be.

Some of the richest people on Earth have mastered the ability to manage time perfectly. They know exactly how much time needs to be spent on a given task. This is why you rarely get to see your CEO as he quite literally has other important things to do. Wasting time talking about things that his managers can handle is not something he is willing to do. To most of us, that is simply rude as he is not ready to make things better for us individually, but to the CEO, that means he has more time to do something that can improve the entire corporation. Slice it any way you like, but I prefer the way of the CEO, a small sacrifice for a greater good.

So, what exactly should you start doing to manage your time accordingly? Here are some of the finest tips I have come across in my life and worked upon to help me improve my situation.

Learn How To Spend Your Time

Sometimes, striking a balance between work, family and a bit of 'me' time is hard. Most of us are providing more time to one of these three than we need to. No offense, but the fact is simple: Spending too much time with family or spending too much time on your own can greatly affect your work and those around you. If you lose your job, your family would face hardships, and to avoid that, we need to ensure we provide the right amount of time to work. The rest of the day can be divided for family and for yourself.

If it helps, maintain a time log and record your activities. After every hour, record an entry and jot down whatever you did within that hour. By the end of the week, reflect on this logbook and find a pattern that truly works for you. At the same time, watch out for things that serve as a distraction, especially during your work hours. Once you have identified those, try your best to keep such distractions away from you during specific hours.

The logbook also provides you a chance to learn how to plan more effectively as you will learn how long it takes for you to do something. Now, you can further utilize time to be more productive. Knowing that a task takes 15 minutes, you would immediately know that it should not take an hour. If so, you are either distracted or not paying much attention.

Setting Your Priorities

There are tasks that are important, and then there are tasks that are urgent. Learn how to distinguish between the two and then set your priorities accordingly. It is essential for us to know that the most important tasks are not necessarily the most urgent ones. There is a fine line between the two.

The problem arises when you have matters which are seemingly urgent but not important at all. Instead of worrying and spending a significant amount of time on these, we should dedicate a small fraction of time and that is it.

To go about this, keep a "To-Do" list with yourself. You can fill up your list on a daily, weekly or even monthly basis, whichever suits your lifestyle. Start creating your list by either creating sections such as urgent, important and so on, or use color coding to highlight the tasks accordingly. The goal of this list, however, is not to finish the entire list by the end of the designated time. The actual goal for you is to mark off the ones with the highest priority.

This effectively will start revealing things that you may think are important but in reality are not as important. Also, it will help you learn how to prioritize things the way they should be. Expect a few errors at the start, that is how we all learn.

Use Planners

Have you ever seen how, in this day and age, the high earners and extremely wealthy folks use planners? It is strange, yes, but it is mighty effective.

People who resort to using planners, whether physical ones or digital ones are more likely to manage time even more effectively. Unlike most of us, these people value their own time and use planners to mark down dates, venues and times for important or urgent tasks such as board meetings, travel, and even plan things such as vacation and time outs.

The science behind using planners is simple. By recording entries, you no longer need to worry about forgetting what you had to do. A quick look at your planner and you would know what needs to be done. Secondly, you now have a clear mind and do not have to worry about the possibility of forgetting tasks. With a clear mind, you can focus easily on other tasks at hand.

Here are some things you should keep in mind when using a planner:

- Do not record your information elsewhere. Always record it directly on the actual planner itself, whether digital or otherwise. This ensures there is no possibility of losing vital information.

- Review your planner on a daily basis.

- Always carry your planner with you.

- Add the priority list as a part of the planner.

- Keep a backup.

Avoid Multitasking

There was once a time I used to think multitasking was a skill. To be honest, it is a big time-waster. Having more than one task at the same time leaves you with divided attention. This means that you are never truly performing said tasks with the attention they deserve. The result would see these tasks completed with a massive compromise on quality.

As per a recent scientific research (American Psychological Association, 2006), multitasking does not save us time at all. Therefore, the entire concept of handling multiple tasks simultaneously is anything but efficient.

Stay Healthy

Okay, this surprised me as well. However, it quickly made sense later on. As long as we are healthy, we can get the job done in an efficient and effective manner. If we lose our health, or are feeling a bit down, we may lose focus or be unable to carry out physical tasks efficiently. Therefore, the overall time spent on a task would increase significantly. What you could have done in four hours may now take twice that.

Stay Organized

Quite a lot of issues we face at work, or even at home, are due to being disorganized. When we worry about where we store our things, or about putting them back where we picked them from, we waste valuable time when we really need to get the job done.

Professionals at work especially need to work on this skill. Learn how to remain organized and categorize important things accordingly. Keep what is important close to you while all that is not important away. Start decluttering your workspace and home as well. Discard or give away anything that is unneeded and retain what is essential.

For handling information at work, you can do these five things to help you manage time:

- Discard, throw it away or delete if it is useless.

- Ask someone else to look into it, when possible.

- File it or throw it, but act on it yourself.

- File it for now under "follow up" labels, on a temporary basis, to the point where it needs some action. Once done, remove it.

- File it for good for later access. This is for information that is required over and over again.

With these tips and habitual changes, you should feel things are decluttered within a month. I promise you, the results are well worth the wait.

Managing time effectively greatly helps us get closer to our goal of being rich. After all, we are trying to be wealthy or rich so that we can spend time the way we see fit. Yes, the investment and post-retirement income do matter, but nothing takes precedence over time.

Lastly, as far as planning is concerned, I would certainly advise to reserve a section in your "To-do" list for yearly targets. It does not matter how you carry out your tasks and in what order. The entire exercise will allow you to plan ahead and by the end of the year, it should allow you to reflect on how much of said targets and goals you have achieved. Without setting goals and targets, one can never truly measure success.

Once you get the hang of things, aim for a longer list, one that spans to a few years from now. Jot down what you must acquire or accomplish by the end of the given period. It will automatically allow you to focus on things, save money where needed, and dedicate specific time accordingly.

This then wraps up the prerequisites; it is now time to start learning about things that you can and must do to start walking on the path that leads to the realization of your goals.

Chapter 4: Freedom - A Must Have For All

Freedom is a gift to mankind. Regardless of where on Earth you are, freedom is all around us, or at least this is what we think. For a day to cherish freedom, you spent countless hours throughout the week, just so you could earn your rightful freedom for the weekend. This changes everything, especially if you have never truly given freedom a thought.

We may live in a country that acquired its freedom hundreds of years ago, but that does not mean that we are free to do whatever we please, does it?

We wake up every morning at a specific time, get ready and leave for work. We need to work for hours every day before leaving the workplace and catching a ride back home. Then, we are bound by responsibilities such as paying taxes, paying our bills, not to mention sacrificing a whole lot just so we can meet our deadline for that project assigned by our bosses. Where is the freedom in that?

Freedom is a birthright for every person alive today. However, our society is designed to teach us how to enslave ourselves to a system that knows only how to exploit us humans. The irony is that all the great universities and institutes prepare us to get a better job so that we can pay more in exchange for a life close to what we wish to lead, that too at the expense of our time. Freedom, then, seems more of a fading concept.

True freedom would see us living life without worries about how we will spend the rest of our day, where we would spend it and how. Truthfully speaking, the native seamen of Vietnam enjoy far more freedom than we do despite having no connection to land or money. They quite literally are born in a raft at sea, grow up there and die there as well. On extremely rare occasions, they step foot on land.

So where is our freedom then? As it turns out, everyone in this world must earn their own freedom. To a person, freedom might be the day they retire from work. To some, freedom might be to relocate to a completely remote city or island, where they can set up a small business and spend the rest of their lives happily. The meaning varies from person to person, however, one thing remains constant for us all: a change of lifestyle.

In order to acquire freedom, quite a lot needs to change in our lives. We need to change the way we work, the way we live and cut down all the additional, and frankly unnecessary responsibilities we tend to take up along the way. To help us achieve that, here are a few things you can start working on right away.

Learn How To Say No

Everyone on Earth is leading a life on their own terms. Whatever they gain, they gain it for themselves. Similarly, whatever they lose, it affects only them. With that in mind, try and remember that you too are trying to lead a life and work your way to the point where you can realize your dream. Taking on additional responsibilities would either slow your progress down to a halt or completely bring everything to an abrupt stop.

Start with simple things. The next time someone asks you to take care of an assignment for them, simply apologize and let them know you already have quite a lot on your plate. That way, you are not being rude, and you are conveying your message loud and clear. Here's what would happen if you say yes:

- The assignment is completed and someone else gets to take all the credit whereas you only get a quick wink. Productive or fruitful? Not really!

- The assignment is delayed and hence the person would start behaving rudely, telling you on how they trusted you with something important and how you couldn't handle such a simple task.

Either way, it is neither important nor beneficial to you in any way. Steer clear of such colleagues and superiors, and continue to focus on your own tasks only.

By doing so, you are ensuring that you do not sacrifice your own time by taking on additional responsibilities. You can now use that time effectively to work or even make room for some leisure time after work.

Have Your Say

There are things that happen at home or at work, and as it turns out, quite a lot of them are imposed upon us. While the working environment has different dynamics, you might still see things happening which you do not approve of, such as nepotism, unjustified actions, discrimination or unjust favors for others. The sooner you start using your voice, the sooner you can bring some changes.

This especially helps if you are married or live with a partner. I have seen quite a lot of examples where one is always calling the shots while the other is obeying them. When asked why they don't let the partner know that they do not approve of this or find this feasible, they remained silent.

There is no reason to fear your partner nor feel guilty for letting your opinions out. If you are a part of a relationship where all the matters regarding the house and life in general are being dictated, and your voice is being ignored, I hate to break it to you but you need to either change the way things work or move on completely. Freedom starts from your home, and if you are not allowed to carry out certain wishes, tasks, or changes, you aren't a free person. Learn how to use your voice to let yourself be heard. While doing so, it is good to hear the other party out. A healthy discussion can often bring out a third option that might be of interest to both parties.

Your voice matters, and it is a vital cog that needs to be there in order to acquire freedom. Without it, freedom is a distant dream.

Stop Fearing The Unknown

One of the biggest hurdles in the path to success is the unknown. Most of us flee from the mere thought of what might happen if something goes wrong or how it would change life if things do not work out. Those who succeed are known to be bold and confident. They take risks just like us, but unlike us, they stick to their plans and actions. We tend to buckle under the pressure and let go of the idea of venturing to uncharted waters.

To truly taste what freedom feels like, you will be facing quite a lot of challenges in life. Rest assured that many of them would require you to take risks and step into the unknown. As long as you remain focused and confident, you will achieve your tasks and come out a more improved person. For those who are left behind, things will only get tougher for them. The sooner you learn to buckle up and make the most of the situation, the sooner you can realize the rewards.

Some important benefits you will get by mustering the courage to face the so-called unknown include:

- Ability to take chances in life
- Finding more courage to do things in life
- A wide variety of experiences
- Find more meaningful peace
- Becoming wiser
- Becoming more comfortable with your own self
- Clearing out uncertainty
- Healthier self-esteem

- Ability to meet more people easily
- Fulfill more dreams than ever before
- Do the things you never thought possible
- Gain more motivation
- Live more freely

And that, by any standard, is quite a list of benefits.

This is something you would want to start working on as soon as you can, because to truly earn a free lifestyle and enjoy freedom, you would either need to invest into some form of business or invest in index funds, savings account and pursue something completely different. The biggest freedom we can have as professionals is freedom from work. Freedom to do the kind of work we actually enjoy.

Freedom From Work

Since I touched upon the topic of investing in a business or setting up your own base, regardless of the place, you need all the courage and determination you can get, along with the finances needed as well. Many have all the financial support in the world, but due to their lack of confidence or ability to cope with others, they never get to see the light at the end of the tunnel.

There was a time even I doubted quite a lot of things. It was only after I started reading some motivational books and stories that I started revisiting my doubts and fears. Before I knew it, I was doing things I never thought I would be able to do on my own. One of those things I always feared was whether my writing would merit anyone's attention. Soon enough, I started writing more freely as I no longer had this nagging doubt within my mind.

Now, I know what I need to do, how I should do it, and I know I will be satisfied with a job I know I can do well. To me, working on my own for something I am passionate about, is beyond any freedom I can ask for. I can choose when I want to write, where I want to write and on what topic I wish to write. Had I been in a firm, I would be doing things under direct orders and dictations, and that is not my idea of freedom or work itself.

"The great revolution in the history of man, past, present and future, is the revolution of those determined to be free." - John F. Kennedy

There are two ways you can get freedom from work. You can either say goodbye to your job altogether and start your own venture, which is perhaps the most obvious choice for most, or work in a field where your heart lies.

To quite a few, it has been a dream to work in a specific field. We know we have what it takes to do some kind of a job far better than the one we are currently doing. You may be a sales manager, but you know you can do exceptionally well in marketing. How about seeking a possible career in the field of graphic designing or web development?

While all of that sounds pleasing, the fact remains that we are far too afraid to make that jump. We are bogged down by so many questions, fear and pressures that we simply let these dreams slide. It is only when someone else who mustered up some courage and made the jump, and made it big that we feel let down and depressed.

Here is the simple formula in life that I have recently picked up on: Do something in life you are passionate about. Take away the passion and you are only left with work.

No one likes working, however, for those who work in a field they are passionate about, it is a completely different story altogether.

Work and passion, if combined, change everything. What may seem monotonous and repetitive to many would now seem increasingly interesting every day. This applies to every single field you can imagine.

If you are someone who loves to create music, you can quite literally let your creativity loose and explore the magical world, with almost no pressure or the typical work anxiety. Ask someone else to join in who may not share the same passion as you, and that person would only be working for the sake of it.

Find the passion that drives and makes you want to achieve more, and you will experience freedom of a different kind. This kind allows you to seek your passion, and continue to earn a good amount. You will quite literally never feel like you are working a typical desk job, where you constantly are pushed by deadlines, confusing situations and a sense of worry about not understanding what exactly needs to be done.

Imagine doing something you love and being paid for it. This kind of freedom is simply unparalleled.

"If the freedom of speech is taken away then dumb and silent we may be led, like sheep to the slaughter." - George Washington

It is only natural that you find peace in doing something that connects to your inner self while you feel bothered, burdened and frankly irritated doing something you 'need' to do instead.

Achieving this only requires you to change the way you think about work. Ask yourself one simple question, would you continue to work if the work stopped paying you? I would not be surprised if your answer is no.

As per a research conducted by Gallup Research, more than 70% of people work to get paid. They have zero interest in the work itself and are always out to seek better opportunities (Sorenson, 2013). The remainder is where we want to be.

To do that, start exploring your interests and passions. Although, by this age, you should be well aware of what truly interests you, however, it is never too late to sit down and have a bit of a think over what you would truly be comfortable with.

Once you have discovered that incredible talent or passion of yours, it is time to set the gears in motion and start searching for an opportunity. If you are someone with a bit of technical skills, you might even try your hand at freelancing. With enough exposure to various projects, you may stand a good chance of starting your own little venture, with virtually no investment.

The great thing about passion at work is that you get to enjoy numerous benefits and advantages which you may never experience in your regular job. To give you an idea of what you are missing out on, here are some of the most reported reasons why people have switched from their regular jobs to doing something they are passionate about:

- **It helps to increase your focus** - Add work and passion together, and you are more attentive and focused than ever before. You pay the perfect attention to matters and have a complete focus on things you need to do.

- **It paves way for innovation and creativity** - With virtually no pressure or lack of interest, you know well what you need to do. With a focused mind, you are able to pursue creativity and innovation at newer heights. Doing things like never before, you will continue to learn and develop to find even better, more creative and innovative ways to carry out your tasks.

- **A renewed desire for excellence** - Unlike in other situations, you will always be pursuing better ways to aim for excellence and hence will put in your best every single time.

- **Increased contribution** - By doing something you are passionate about, there is no such thing as enough, and you are constantly and happily engaged in working more. The resulting output will see your productivity rise many folds.

- **Renewed energy** - Whether you are 26 or 40, passion automatically brings a source of energy that never depletes. You would always find yourself doing things more effectively and with more determination. No longer do you have to wake up with a frown. Instead, you now rise with a goal you are more than happy to pursue.

- **Passion motivates you** - One of the biggest drawbacks in professional life is the lack of motivation. Here though, the passion alone serves as a huge motivator. It is also proven that passionate folks tend to be a class apart when it comes to productivity and professionalism.

- **Less stress, more satisfaction** - At the end of a long day, you arrive home with a smile, knowing that you did something worth your effort and time. While stress may still be around, it would be significantly lower.

- **No such thing as workload** - Every task that comes your way is yet another opportunity for you to impress yourself and your clients or bosses.

- **Passion improves work environment** - It is a fact that a passionate team will always outshine every other team. Working with people who are passionate will always improve the overall environment at work. That means you end up with more work done and almost no quarrels or conflicts at work.

There are many other advantages, and I can go on for pages and pages, however, they are best if experienced personally.

Your ultimate aim is to seek that freedom you so truly desire. No book on earth would claim that freedom comes after work. There are those who find freedom at work as well. Imagine saving enough money to buy a decent place in the countryside and living worry-free, knowing that you can grow all the food you ever need, with all the resources you can possibly require and an amazing view to surrounding yourself with. As appealing as that sounds, you still need to put in some efforts to manage your farm and gardens.

There are many great ways through which you can settle down, enjoy your time and freedom. Unfortunately, most of them require you to take some leap of faith, and a bit of investment as well. This then leads to a problem; where exactly should you start? What if you do not have a massive six-figure sum lying around that you can use?

Things continue to change at a rapid pace in today's world. No longer do you need to learn all the tricks of the trade. A quick look over the internet and you can quickly establish a good understanding of how things might work in a specific field.

Start by looking for small investment opportunities which offer a reasonable return on investment (ROI). Usually, a good rate is around 10% to 15% per annum. Depending on what you aim to invest in, how much you are looking to invest and the duration of your investment, your returns and ROI figures may vary.

Your first dollar as an investment should not be expected to make any return. It is usually for the sake of getting our feet wet and gaining our first-ever experience of how things work and what might have gone wrong. With this in mind, make sure you do not invest a large sum on your first attempt.

These petty investments have good potential to grow into a significant amount over a short period of time. With multiple investments, you can start reaping profits or reinvest the same to further increase your returns. Eventually, with the right investments, you should start making enough to save four figures every month, and that does not include your current salary that you may be saving.

Do not consider the profits and the increased savings as your reward, the actual reward lies when you make enough money to actually buy a piece of property, a running business or anything that can provide you a perpetual source of earning and the freedom that comes along when you know you do not need to work as someone's employee anymore. The road is quite a stretch, but the second you take your first step, everything will start falling into place. Before you know it, you would be looking back and thanking yourself for making such a decision that eventually changed your life.

Some Good Investment Ideas

Some of my friends have invested their savings in various fields. Most of them learned from their experiences while some made profits in the first go. Despite all that, everyone picked up some tips and tricks and are now drawing good profits on a monthly basis. It might sound surprising but these friends decided to browse through the internet and list down some ideas for their next investments, and they actually worked in the long run. Here are some of the ideas and venues where you can start with small investments:

- Savings Accounts
- Robo Advisors (e.g. Betterment)
- Lending Club
- Mutual Funds
- Online Brokerage Firms
- Domain Trading
- Website Flipping
- Dropshipping

Most of these require as little as $50 to begin. The returns can often surprise you with the margin of profits. For the tech-savvy readers, there is a world full of opportunities out there. The more you search, the more you find.

Finally, you can start investing in your own miniature business model. Start as a single person and make things happen. There are many who started out as a one-man army and ultimately converted their small venture into a money-making machine. Depending on the type of skill you may have, such as drawing, photography, website designs, you can start gathering work and selling your services to make a good side hustle. Once you see it gaining pace, and it is fetching you enough money to cover your expenses, let go of your day time job and make this into your next full-time commitment, one that will last you the rest of your life.

Start hiring the right people, start your own small business model and be the boss you always wanted to be. Control how things work and find that freedom that it comes with. There is nothing more satisfying than a productive day at work, which you happen to own.

Procrastination Is Not Freedom

There are times in life where you feel like you can use a bit of a break from work and then there are times in life where you take a break from work when you really don't need to. The former is acceptable, and even science suggests a break is vital. The latter on the other hand is one that can cause quite a lot of problems. That is simply laziness and lack of motivation, wrapped up in a result called procrastination.

If you are someone who often feels like you can delay a certain task for a bit, and that it would not affect the outcome at all, you are most likely procrastinating matters. I may not be able to predict everyone's future, but I can certainly guarantee you that procrastination will lead you to all kinds of trouble.

Delaying matters of today would only make tomorrow even tougher. You will begin tomorrow with twice the workload. The extra pressure of being late would cause you to lose your focus and quality. You might be able to get the job done, but that still would not be enough. With a lack of attention to detail, you are going to upset your clients, your bosses and eventually the end-user.

Freedom is knowing you have nothing to worry about and that all has been taken care of. You cannot call procrastination freedom as you are pushing your work further ahead to make room for something you intend to do, such as go to a movie with friends. While you enjoy the movie, the task continues to run out of time and no one is looking after it either. It is only when you come back that you realize the remainder of your day is not enough to cover the task. What happens next is quite obvious.

Make it your rule in life. What needs to be done today must be done today, period. There is no need to find an excuse nor avoid taking responsibility for the delayed work by blaming someone else. It is your work, and hence you alone are responsible for the outcome. Be sure to complete it on time so that you have the capacity to do more things with better quality.

"Procrastination is the thief of time. Collar him!" - Charles Dickens

Those who procrastinate once can usually end up procrastinating far more. The devastating consequences have seen people losing their jobs, their trust, their respect and their professionalism. None of that is going to help you achieve anything in life except disappointment.

I have personally found motivation to be a key component that can allow us to remain focused and away from any distractions. Whatever motivates you, whether it is the leisure time planned after work, a good sleep, the money or even a date, use that throughout the day. Keep reminding yourself that you will earn that after you have done all your tasks as well as you can. Surround your mind with positive quotes, phrases and ornaments which continue to inspire you and motivate you to work even better.

Make it a routine to make today better than yesterday, and I assure you that pretty soon, you will be reigning at the top of your game. Procrastination will only slow you down to a halt. The worst part about procrastination is that it is not limited to your professional life. It can happen at home, at work, on a trip, on a date or pretty much any situation that you can think up of.

If you are starting your own business, procrastinating filling out forms, or delaying reaching out to customers would effectively end up with you losing far more than you can gain. Your reputation would take a nose-dive and that would be a predicament you would not want to face.

Learn how to improve your habits and understand how procrastination and freedom are two different things altogether. Always prioritize work over everything else, unless an absolutely urgent and more important task arises. Setting the right priorities would greatly help you in staying focused and on the right track.

There was a time I used to think people were simply exaggerating on how procrastination can destroy one's career and lifestyle. It was only when I started to experience these consequences that I realized I was wrong.

To give you an idea of just how bad this problem has become, let me paint the picture with some numbers (Gaille, 2017):

- A jaw-dropping 20% of the population is affected by procrastination

- Just within the last three decades, procrastination has quadrupled

- Over 40% of those who procrastinated suffered massive financial losses

- One out of every five people would turn out to be a chronic procrastinator

Procrastination, therefore, is a grim issue, one that needs to be addressed right away before you are too late. This can affect not only your financial standings but your relations as well. If you are worried, or you might have just discovered that you procrastinate as well, do not worry. I have some great tips which you can start working on from now, and these will greatly help you in separating yourself from this horrible ailment.

- Be organized

- Set out goals which are achievable

- Always set deadlines for your tasks

- Say goodbye to distractions

- Where possible, time yourself

- Take a break and then resume work
- Reward yourself or use incentives
- Prioritize the hard stuff and get it done first

Follow these and soon enough, your procrastination days would become a thing of the past. If you truly desire freedom of any kind, whether from work or in the form of retirement, procrastination will push it further back. With that said, now we arrive at the point where we have the foundation laid out. It is now time to focus on your long-term goals, planning the next few years and finding ways to achieve your freedom and that rich lifestyle that eludes many. We will explore various long-term goals, changes and aspects which, if executed correctly, can make all the difference in the world.

Chapter 5: The Long Journey To Freedom

You have your goals set. You know what needs to be done, and you have learned how to avoid procrastinating matters. Yet, you are still hazy on what exactly needs to be done in order to make this dream into a reality.

We all know the road ahead is full of difficulties and trials. It is the kind of path where most have failed for one reason or another and only a select few have walked till the very end to find their success. With so many people who failed, we should have great ease to observe, find and understand what they may have done wrong so that we can avoid doing the same thing, right? Unfortunately, most of us are looking at the wrong end of the picture.

Instead of learning from those who made it, we are more focused on what went wrong with those who didn't get to see the end of the road. Although I do encourage the idea of knowing what possible issues others have faced, I find it more meaningful to ask people who were successful and were able to realize their dreams.

In this chapter, we will be looking at how simple mistakes we make can hold us back from progress and how we can use the knowledge of these to overcome, avoid and hopefully conquer such failures with success. We will look at some significant changes which are essential and play a key part in the making of our success.

There will be some habits we need to let go off, and that might cause some issues in the start. However, remember that we are doing this for a far better life for ourselves and our loved ones. Without these changes, we cannot possibly aim for a better lifestyle, let alone retiring early to lead a life we dream of.

We will also learn about how some of the people around us might be a bad influence on us. We will learn how to identify them and find out ways to ensure we remove them from our social circle. As cruel as this may sound, it is necessary both for work and home that we surround ourselves with motivational and successful people, even if that means to start mingling with that next-door neighbor who always seems to be so smug about his successful lifestyle.

The chapter will also focus on changing our mindset

and our way of looking at things. If you are someone who is constantly living under fear, right now is the time to muster up all the courage you can. Trust me, it will not be easy but it will be worth every second of your time.

The path to your journey begins now; how it ends is absolutely your call!

Making A Commitment

"So far as you continue to entertain what makes you unhappy, you shall always dance to the tune of

what will make you unhappy. A mindset change can cause a great change." - Ernest Agyemang Yeboah

We have made ourselves a promise earlier on. It is time to further strengthen that promise by committing to all that is essential, productive and meaningful while letting go of certain old habits that would otherwise hold us back.

Unknown to many of us, there are quite a lot of things we do on a regular basis and we consider them as friendly or helpful to our cause. The reality, however, is far from that. The only reason we never knew about such things is because no one cared to explain to us the what and the why. We live in a world where we normally overlook the need for going through the details and just jump to the part that is seemingly meaningful.

A simple example can be seen in the quick and easy way of signing contracts, whether for job purposes or acquiring services like cellular services. The terms and conditions hold a lot of information we tend to skip right past by and sign the contract. When certain things fail to go our way, we are left with frustration when we are told we cannot be entertained according to a specific clause or term we agreed to. I am not suggesting you start paying attention to all of these contracts, but start somewhere.

Details hold significant information and allow us to have a clearer view of what to expect should we end up signing said contract. In a similar fashion, there are things in life where we hasten to the end, without worrying about what would happen in the middle. We simply think we would be able to face these circumstances as they come along; and that is a fatal mistake.

Plan To Win

Planning is one of the most important aspects of life. Whether for business or even pleasure, you need to plan things out correctly. Planning involves the use of your intellectual abilities and your skills in foreseeing possible outcomes of a given situation.

In our case, we are aiming for that golden ticket to a rich lifestyle where we would lead without care or worries. Between you and that, however, stands a gray area that we have yet to explore. This isn't a brief period either as most of us might have to work for years or decades before we truly realize our goals and dreams.

Start planning today for a better tomorrow. By planning out your days in advance, you know exactly what needs to be done. The priority list would greatly help us out in knowing what tasks we need to carry out first and which ones can be left out of the equation.

Analyze situations from different angles. Try and change your perspective or have your partner chip in by providing a fresh new take on the task. Just when you might have thought that you know all the possible outcomes, your partner or friend might be able to bring up one undiscovered or unexpected situation. The more you plan for things to come, the better you can handle these situations.

The element of surprise does seem nice but in circumstances where our future is at stake, it is wise and mandatory to keep such surprises as far as possible. Hope for the best but always prepare for the worst as things will continue to change with time. You cannot expect everything to go in a certain direction. There will be times where you might be left stressed out and unable to think clearly. By planning, you minimize such instances or even completely block them out.

Learn To Remain Calm

There are those days in life where everything irritates us. In such instances, it is easy to lose track of what you need to do and lash out at your close friends and family members. The same is the case with professionals. How many times have we seen our bosses losing their cool for no obvious reason and yelling at employees? If it can happen to them, rest assured it can happen to us as well.

To help you change how you deal with emotions, you can work on strengthening your control over your mind and emotions. One of the finest ways to do so is to meditate.

Sure, it does sound monotonous and boring, but it is mighty effective for everyone. All you need is an hour out of your hectic schedule and a meditation technique you prefer. There are hundreds of techniques out there, each allowing you to re-center your focus, regain composure and curb the anger and frustration. After an hour, you quite literally feel brimming with positive energy.

This positive energy will help you in tackling some of the toughest situations life can throw at you, both personally and professionally.

Stop Fearing The Worst

Quite similar to planning for success, it is vital that you stop fearing the worst or the inevitable. If you are a businessman or an employee, chances are that you are working in a field where one day your skills will be rendered obsolete. Instead of fearing that, focus on finding the answer as to what will make that happen.

By realizing the potential hazard that may be just around the corner, you have the chance to change the outcome by acquiring skills or using innovation that can fetch you even better results and keep you one step ahead of others. Not only do you get to secure your job or your profits, but you also get to gain a certain in-demand skill.

Learn new skills as often as you can. These will greatly come in handy when you are ready to retire and lead life the way you prefer. After all, you may still need to have a source of income or some form of engagement to keep your bank account rolling, right? We will get into a little more detail on that in the last chapter.

Change Your Social Circle

It is said that the friends you choose define the kind of a person you are. If you are someone who spends quite a lot of time with people who often find themselves worrying over professional or personal matters, it is quite possible that you too will pick up a thing or two and feel the same way later in life.

One of the biggest secrets behind being successful is to change your active social circle. By surrounding yourself with successful people, you will start seeing things through a new perspective. You will get to learn from the best and find out just how much you have been missing out on.

One great way to get started is to follow what they do through their blogs or by reading their books. Try to analyze how they navigate through their journeys and what makes them unique. There is a good chance that some of these might even be regular speakers at various conferences and seminars.

If luck has it, and such a successful person is sure to visit near you, be sure to attend their seminars. At this point, you might be tempted to meet this person and say hello in person. That is perfectly natural and as it turns out, you might just be able to do that. If you know or have someone who may know them, ask them to introduce you. This is called the drip method and this can often bring some extremely beneficial results.

Learn how they deal with life and learn just how they conquer challenges and obstacles that they may have faced in life. By implementing the same, you will start changing everything about yourself. You will automatically start attracting attention and success will now start chasing you instead of the other way around.

Do not fall for the obvious trap of pitching an idea to them. They have already made it big and may have heard your idea a thousand times. Hear them out and try to build up a rapport and credibility. Soon enough, you just might be able to call them your acquaintances or friends.

This does not stop here, there are many other great ways you can use to get in touch with successful people. These include but are not limited to certain social media platforms, local events, guest appearances and visits.

There may be some ambiguity at the start in knowing who is successful and who poses to be so. With a bit of trial and error, you should soon be able to spot the difference and know whom to follow and draw inspiration from.

Having successful people around you automatically changes quite a lot of things. Just to be around them you know you will need to work on your presentation, your physique, your overall look and your health. You will be brushing up on your skills and knowledge to ensure you are able to maintain a good discussion.

Brush up on your general knowledge and acquire more in-depth information about your relative field as well. There might be instances in the future where your input might be sought; you really wouldn't want to miss out on such an opportunity nor embarrass yourself by being unable to answer accordingly.

If you are someone who may suffer from lack of confidence, start working on your charisma and confidence right away. You will need all that energy in order to make a positive impression. There is a good likelihood that you might come across these select few successful people in parties or social gathering events. You must have a charming personality in order to gain an audience with them and be able to engage in healthy conversations.

Lastly, be as effective of a communicator as you can. Successful people choose their words carefully but still manage to deliver the message clearly across the globe. Knowing what to speak, how to speak and when to speak is your key to attracting some attention.

No More Waiting

There are those who wait for their entire lives for some kind of a magical opportunity that will come and change their lives forever. Then, there are those who just cannot risk waiting for so long and go out to seek such opportunities on their own. Try and take a guess which one ends up succeeding in life; of course, the latter.

Today's highly technologically advanced world of the internet gives us more chances than ever before to go out and seek opportunities, and yet never leave home at all. If you are someone who has a skill or two that is in demand, I can guarantee you can use the internet to gain quite a bit of an audience and, while doing so, make some serious money as well.

If you are passionate about something you do, you can share your experiences with the world through popular streaming websites, and the returns you get are far beyond imaginable. There are numerous success stories that continue to emerge from all corners of the world and these people started with pretty much nothing more than an idea and a moderate computer or camera. Now, they stand as millionaires, and all it took was a decade to change their lives completely.

I am not implying that it is easy, but if you have been following the book so far, you would know it takes time and effort; not to forget consistency. Seek out your passion as you earn handsomely, and you probably would retire far quicker than you can realize.

Apart from streaming or posting videos online, you can also take up writing blogs and community forums such as Quora and Reddit. These are some of the biggest names in existence and serve as great platforms to gain a global audience. You can use that audience to further benefit you by referring them to your affiliate links for more sales, or by selling your own services directly.

The world of the internet is just a click away. There remains no reason for anyone to delay the matter any longer as now you do not have to travel half-way across the Earth to pursue a possible opportunity. Simply search for what you are looking for, gather information and start doing what needs to be done.

Even freelancers are making six-figure salaries per year while being in the comfort of their homes. If working at home feels a little strange, set up a simple office in rented premises. Hire like-minded people and start selling your services to your esteemed clients.

The world is changing rapidly and it is far easier now than it has ever been before to seek out your next venture. Adapting to this change might be a bit tricky, especially if you are someone who has no idea on how to operate computers, but there is still a lot of time remaining for you to learn, develop and make something out of this newly found frontier.

Stop The Negativity

Throughout your life, you will cross paths with people who are just too eager to tell you how miserable you are and how you will lead to failure. The minute you start paying attention to these people and their opinions, you will invite negativity within yourself.

Negativity will continue to chase us until our last breath. Decide whether you wish to succumb to it and lose everything or rise above it and lead as a determined person. Always know that you are pursuing the goals that you believe in only for yourself. Whether you end up becoming a millionaire or not, these people will hardly be affected.

Stop feeding your mind with negative thoughts and stop doubting yourself. If you procrastinate matters, I assure you that you will ultimately start feeling bad about yourself. Instead of searching around for a way out, change your habits. Stop feeling sorry and depressed and stop procrastinating. You will soon learn just how rewarding it can be to invest your time in something productive and meaningful rather than wasting your time in something that could have been done any given day.

Focusing On Yourself

From the start, I have gone through various examples, numerous situations and who knows how many key components, but one thing stands constant: you!

This entire journey is about you. If you stop paying attention to yourself, there is no journey to begin with. There will certainly be no realization of the dream if you stop paying attention to yourself, your hygiene, your health and your well-being.

No one can take care of you better than your own self. Even if you are married, understand that your partner can only know what he/she can see, feel or hear. What goes on within your mind, what you might be worried about and the things you cannot share remain within you.

These can greatly harm you and hamper your progress towards your ultimate goal. It is, therefore, of utmost importance that you start taking out time for yourself and start allowing your body, mind and soul to feel energized, alive and positive. How we go about that is far easier than you might imagine.

Start Seeking Knowledge

I am not referring to novels and storybooks, I am genuinely referring to knowledgeable sources that can teach you a thing or two at the end. An average CEO reads around 60 books a year. It is not because they are habitual readers, but purely for the purpose of learning.

Develop that curiosity within yourself to learn something new throughout the year. You can use a planner and set goals accordingly to learn something every month that you can use to further enhance your personal and professional life.

These days you can pick up a book for just about anything. Filter out the unnecessary ones and focus on skills and abilities which you believe would help you make things better for yourself. If you are not good with money, start reading about financial management, budgeting or investment tips and tricks. If you fancy creating websites or applications, start learning about web development, programming and so on.

If you are aiming for long-term learning, there are plenty of options available such as artificial intelligence, machine learning, and books about business ideas and emerging business ventures which can perhaps provide you an edge over your competitors. The process of learning is one that never stops. Do not allow yourself to be bogged down thinking that you know enough. There is no such thing as "too much knowledge" as something becomes obsolete every day and is replaced by something new altogether. Keep up with the trend and be a step ahead.

Such knowledge will help you in achieving quite a lot more in life, and even when you have finally gathered all the experience, ideas, resources and finances to settle.

Start Focusing On Your Health

Health; Without it, there is no wealth. And that is a fact no one can dispute.

If you are healthy, you can achieve everything. If you are unwell, you would struggle to even carry out simple tasks like walking to the bathroom or taking a stroll down your lane, let alone conquering challenges and staying at the top of the food chain.

Start eating a healthy diet and couple that with regular exercise. A typical successful person would wake up early in the morning for a walk before they decide to settle down for a shower and a hearty breakfast. Walking is good for your body and mind. It allows you to recover all the lost stamina while toning your body to a perfect shape. If you have a few extra pounds on you, this is a great way to shed them as well.

Focus on your health and maintain your physique by avoiding unnecessary trips in vehicles. Instead, take a walk and soak in the fresh air around you. Your legs might feel sore in the first week, but once they get used to it, your body will start craving for exercise itself. Wash all the sweat away with a relaxing shower and then carry on with the rest of the day as usual. Not only will your body feel fresh, but you will feel calm and ready to take on the day.

Exercises are also a great way to reduce stress levels. Too much stress can not only harm your mind but it can have a devastating effect on your health as well. There are many diseases and ailments which will plague you if you are constantly feeling stressed out. Avoid the stress and rely on a good walk to sort out most of the stresses right away.

Personal Grooming

Have you ever noticed how successful people are always well dressed and look sharp? That is because they know how important it is to keep themselves groomed every single day.

Focusing on your personal grooming can bring positive results instantly. People notice these tiny but significant changes within you. If you have a beard, trim it neatly. If you have long hair, either go for a trim or style it in a sleek manner that compliments your dress and personality.

Do not rely on flip flops for the day. Instead, do the extra work and wear shoes or trainers which suit the occasion. Keep in mind that how you look reflects the kind of person you are.

There is a reason why superstar Christiano Ronaldo disguised himself as a street beggar by putting on a shabby beard and messy hair. People automatically started walking in the other direction because they did not like what they were seeing. The minute he took his disguise off, people immediately surrounded him.

It goes to show that your physical appearance is all that matters in the day. When you are with friends, with colleagues, at work or even traveling, be sure to step out of the house in your best appearance. Success finds people who care more about their grooming than those who overlook its importance.

Needs Over Desires

We have all been there, where we walked across a shop and stopped immediately to admire something that was just on the other side of the thick glass.

Whether a guitar, a camera or even a laptop, we knew we wanted one and we went ahead to buy it. Hardly a few months later, we then start aiming for something else and this purchase of ours starts gathering dust in some remote corner of the house. To me, and to all successful people, that is a waste of money, time and resources.

Yes, we desire a great many things in life, but everything in life has its time and place. Right now, our focus is to achieve that lifestyle where we will never be worried about our purchases or the way we spend our days. To achieve that truly, we must learn how to let go of our temptations and stop paying attention to them.

If you have a phone and a new version comes out in the market, stop rushing to the nearest store to buy it. You already have a phone that works just as fine. Do not let temptation get the best of you.

Stick to the concept of minimalism, live with little to make room for more!

By learning how to suffice with the things you have, you only start focusing on what you need and overlook anything that might be nothing more than a burden on the pocketbook. This way, you would be saving up faster than ever before. Even the initially discussed concept of FIRE revolves around the same. This is indeed effective but takes a lot of effort to maintain.

What we have learned so far should carry you forward a bit, but when does it end? We will now move on to our final chapter to discover "Are we there yet?"

Chapter 6: Creating Your Own Future

A few years down the road, you will feel the change around you. Everything seems to be heading right where and how you had imagined. You feel better, you are able to perform your tasks with more determination and purpose, and your goal is drawing closer than ever before. The path you had started on, it is now taking a promising shape. However, there is still much that needs to be done in order to ensure you stay on track and, where possible, speed up the process a little to taste that sweet feeling of achievement sooner.

Well, fortunately, there are certain things you can do to make that happen. To get you going in the right direction a little faster, you would need to work on a few things and improve them as much as possible.

Most of these things are simply old habits, and if history has taught us anything, we human beings have a tendency of falling back for those habits even after years of resistance.

I discussed how important health is for anyone who is trying to make it big in the end. Unfortunately, quite a few of us resort to bad habits which deteriorate our health conditions. These habits can include but are not limited to:

1. Smoking
2. Alcohol
3. Laziness

4. Staying up late
5. Waking up late
6. Sleeping too little or too much
7. Addictions (drugs and narcotics)
8. Excessive use of electronics such as cell phones and tablets

Any of these would and could affect the outcome of your struggle. If you smoke too much, you risk running into life-threatening diseases like cancer. If you are someone who prefers to stay up late at night for pleasure or work, it will take a toll on your body and bring your focus and energy levels down the next day. The list goes on and on.

Excess of anything is bad, and at this point in time, bad is what we really do not wish to have around us. For that perfect retirement, it is vital that we take every possible measure to keep anything that can harm our chances away from our professional and personal lives. With that said however, these are not the only things you need to worry about. There is plenty more where that came from. The good news is, by the end of this chapter, you already know what to look out for and plan your moves accordingly.

Avoiding The Obvious Traps

The journey to living a truly rich life is full of perils, competition and challenges. Whether we like it or not, we will eventually have to face each and every one of them. But the biggest issues are the ones which are far too obvious that we easily overlook. We are looking out for what we believe are bigger issues to worry about whereas these small ones have enough power to devastate our efforts and take that goal further away from us. It is therefore time to get to know what exactly are these traps and how we can avoid them to succeed in life.

Not Seeking Help

Throughout your journey, you will come across various situations which would either pose a challenge or a threat. Depending on the circumstances, you will always have options to choose from. The real problem would be our ego which would not allow us to seek help from other professionals. To an ordinary person, this would mean throwing in the towel and calling it quits.

Let us look at Bill Gates, one of the richest people on Earth. The guy who single-handedly created an empire worth billions of dollars and became a monopoly for a very long time. His vision of an operating system dominated the world and continues to do so. Almost every other computer we buy comes pre-installed with Microsoft Windows. However, for the non-technical people, here is a dose of some technical side for you.

Developing an operating system (OS) is no easy task. It takes millions of coded lines to be written by experts before they can even testrun an OS. Bill Gates certainly did come up with the OS but he never did it alone. If he had been someone with a bit of an ego and had he not asked for professional assistance in handling these matters, the world today would have never known Microsoft or Windows for that matter. Bill Gates would have been just another name in the heap of files, lost in the dark and forgotten section of some public library.

Seeking professional assistance can often get you out of some extremely difficult situations. There is a reason giant corporations employ or outsource experts to resolve their issues. You cannot possibly think of succeeding in life if you let your ego make your decisions. As long as you are true to your goal and you have a clear sight of what needs to be done, ego will never find its way to you.

Seek out professional assistance where necessary. For bosses and CEOs, they hire professionals to do the groundwork while they focus on larger-scale issues. Similarly, allow someone else to use their expertise to get results you desire while you focus on more important tasks at hand. Remember, there will always be people who are better at a specific skill than you. Life is not a race to prove you are better.

Settling For Less

While the entire minimalist approach is indeed a gift and a blessing in disguise, it does not mean that you should also start to lose opportunities or start selling your expertise and skills for less. The day you start doing that, you are not only unfair towards others of equal skills, but you are also being unfair to your own self as well.

I have seen hundreds and thousands of such cases where people start selling their services for far less than their worth. The problem is that with such low wages and rates, the other deserving candidates and prospects never get the exposure they need. Why should I care? I am making money, aren't I?

What might seem like a money-making move will quickly turn into a permanent burden to endure. Once you start charging low, you will never be able to make enough money to expand properly. Furthermore, you will be burdened by a mountain of workload and eventually you will start feeling irritated for being paid so less against your efforts. The result will eventually lead you to become least interested in what you are doing, a lack of focus on what you might be working on and a displeased client who will eventually start spreading negative reviews about you. Not only would you end up losing your contacts and clients, but you will hit a dead-end. The only person to blame here is you.

If you know your skills are unique and matter, remain market competitive. Whether picking up a job offer or working solo as a businessman or a freelancer, do thorough research about how much a person would make on average with the same job description as you. Never settle for a lesser amount as that would take away the motivation from work and leave you with a feeling of being imprisoned by work.

Keep Your Goals In Sight

With life's sheer unpredictable nature, it is easy to get distracted and go off course. This can happen to anyone and no human being on Earth is immune to such temptations and attractions. Tackling this one then, is anything but easy.

When aiming for a more secure future, there will come a time where you might forget how much you have saved. One fine day, you will be taken by surprise to see the big numbers within your bank account. At such moments, you can easily be distracted into thinking you can use that money to take a long vacation or buy that brand-new car on the market. My advice would be simple: Stop!

Think matters through and understand how your decision can affect the outcome. Your long-term goal can easily be jeopardized by the unexpected withdrawals from your account. Think about how your current situation can be brought down by spending such a large chunk of money on things you may not need at all.

If you are someone who uses public transport, stick to it for now. Even Keanu Reeves, the star who played Neo in The Matrix movies uses public transport and his rides are normally motorbikes instead of flashy cars like a Ferrari or a Pagani. If he can do that, so can you.

Focus on the ultimate goal in life and do whatever it takes to stay true to your course. Temptations will come and go day in and day out. You can indulge in these as much as you like once you have everything set up and you have reached your destination the way you had hoped.

Never Give Up

Easier said than done. I wish there was a way to make things a bit easier for everyone, but, unfortunately, we all have to face situations where we feel like we have hit rock bottom.

The biggest contributors are the people around us who have never experienced the kind of success we are aiming for. This is one reason why I suggested you start mingling with successful people. I do not intend to sound rude, but you will need to draw a line in the sand and let everyone know what you can tolerate and what you prefer them not to comment on.

Opinions, suggestions and criticism coming from people who have never done anything or achieved the sort of success you aim for serves to do nothing more than shatter your morale. These can harm you and leave you in an emotionally wrecked state. Recovering from such a state will take time and as we have discussed, time is a luxury we cannot afford to lose.

In such situations, learn how to respectfully let the other party know you are not looking for criticism or interested in entertaining suggestions. As long as you know what needs to be done, you do not need to pay attention to what others have to say. Motivate yourself from the fact that you are hoping to lead by example so that one day the very same people who are busy criticizing you will get up and say "I know that person!" That is your prize and the moment of victory to see that you were able to silence the critics and stand out against all the odds as a defiant winner.

Knowing When You Are There

The arduously long and testing journey will eventually come to an end, but how exactly do we know when we are there? Are we to expect some kind of a signboard that says, "You made it!" or a dream where some voice tells us this is it?

The answer to this completely depends on what your vision of living on holiday is. To some, it might come a little sooner while to others it may take a while. However, if you have set out realistic goals, it won't take long before you realize you have made it.

The numbers in your savings account would match, the people around you would applaud and praise your efforts, the world would open its embrace to you and success would seem to follow you everywhere you go. That is when you know you have truly made it to the point you once dreamed of.

Knowing that you have now made it through, the biggest question that comes to mind is, "What's next?"

Do What You Have Always Wanted to Do

Ever dream of living on a remote and exotic island with a small bar facing the beach? Perhaps you dreamed of buying a house in the remote countryside and growing your own stock of food. Whatever the dream, now is the time to implement that. You have already gone through the hardest part of life. What lies ahead should be a piece of cake.

With the rich experience, all the skills you picked up and the knowledge you gathered from your colleagues and books, enable you to do anything with your life. Money, at least now, would honestly not matter as much as it may have a few years ago. You have retired and have invested some amount in a savings account or some kind of stocks. You know you can continue to draw from those profits and only use the savings itself to set up camp and small business to keep your needs fulfilled.

It is time to put on a hat, sit on a beach chair, with a pint of your favorite beer, and savor the moment. If you are someone who prefers to continue working, sit behind the counter of your small business and have a team of employees carry out the operation while you enjoy the fruits of your hard work. No longer do you have to worry about meeting deadlines or staying up late at night to finish off assignments. You do not need to be dictated to anymore and are free to lead exactly the kind of life you had imagined. The best part is, you are still young enough and were able to retire far earlier than the national retirement age, allowing you to cherish life to the fullest.

Reflect Back on Your Journey

One of the best things in life is when you look back in life and see where you started from, you are immediately met with this sense of accomplishment. You are happy as you remind yourself how you were once worried about how everything would turn out to be, and now everything has turned out just fine. You can now spend quality time with your family every day and enjoy your time with kids, take them to the park or for a quick swim at the beach, and you know you can do that because you have worked so much for it. You have earned yourself the right to buy yourself this quality time.

And just when you think things can't get any better, you realize you have become a self-made man. You did not rely on anyone's favor nor did you ask for financial assistance from anyone. Whatever you have, you are happy and grateful. Whatever you will now buy, you will cherish it far more than you may have done before. Remember the phones and the cars? Go ahead, knock yourself out and have a blast.

Lead By Example

With such success comes the responsibility of being a responsible leader. Your story will be one that everyone will hear about. Everyone who might be starting to realize their goals will now seek out your advice, even the people who once discouraged you would hope for your time and valuable words of wisdom.

Lead by example and set the bar high for everyone else. Let others know how they can achieve anything in life as long as they truly believe in themselves and their goals. Let them know how, without falling for any illegal matters, they can lead a life that is worth the hard work.

Continue to Invest Wisely

While you have a business that continues to generate some good profits, it is wise to continue investing wisely to further add to your savings account. You can pick up the latest stocks, hire a brokerage firm to handle your investments or simply start investing in properties. I would personally recommend buying apartments and renting them out as that would draw a monthly income and appreciate in value at the same time.

You can enjoy the rental income for a year or two, sell for a profit and buy another one. You can repeat the cycle as many times as you like, and you will still end up making profits every single month.

Your Ultimate Reward

Finally, with your finances and work sorted, it is time to sit back, relax, go on a vacation, hang out with friends and enjoy life for what it is. Live a truly rich life that you defined for yourself. With nothing left to do, you have everything else to experience now!

Conclusion

Life is brief, and before you know it, you would be reflecting back at how quickly time went by. You can either be someone who stands by and watches as time flies, or you can be someone who works against all the odds to come out as a worthy champion. Either way, time will continue to tick away.

While we cannot control time, there are, however, things we can certainly control, and one of them is how our future is going to be. As silly as it may sound, it is actually possible. We have gone through so much, from the beginning of the book right till the very last chapter, and we have learned to pursue this dream. A dream of a life where finances, worries, deadlines and work pressure is nowhere to be seen. A life where what we do is not a decision enforced upon us by time or peer pressure but purely through our own will. Such a life was once only a dream for many, but with the right tools and knowledge, it is already looking like something a little more realistic.

Achieving the impossible is possible. All it takes is the right mindset, nerves of steel and determination.

To keep us going, we need to do quite a bit of homework to make the journey a little easier. Some of the things we need are:

- Realistic planning
- Realistic goals
- Achievable targets
- Foreseeing possible issues
- Letting go of the bad and accepting the good
- Learning how to take a stand and say no

We have maneuvered throughout the book and tackled various situations. The purpose behind going through all of that was simple; to know what exactly is expected on the journey ahead. The earlier you know, the more time you have to plan accordingly.

We learned that the greatest and most valuable luxuries we have are time and our health. Without either of the two, we will simply cease to exist. As long as we remain healthy and we have the time, we need to utilize it productively to close in on the goal we have set for ourselves.

Achieving the goal would require some sacrifices, such as letting go of time-wasting distractions, and certain changes, such as socializing more with successful people. The long journey ahead would teach us quite a lot through various exposures and experiences. These will exactly be what we need to ensure our success.

As the journey goes on, there will be the possibility we might hit a dead-end. There is no shame in retracing your steps a little and learning from your mistakes. Quitting, however, is not an option. To succeed in life, we must learn how to find motivation and keep our morale high. Giving up is the way of quitters and that is not what we are. In order to fully utilize the opportunity, constant striving to become better requires us to be ready, and willing to learn and never give up.

After all these changes and years of hard work, the fruits of your labor will finally be ready for the picking. How you spend your days then is absolutely your call. No one can and no one will dictate your life; you may lead it as you please.

Remember, the journey of a thousand miles starts with the first step. The sooner you take it, the sooner you will reach your destination. Wherever you may be on God's green Earth,

References

Cherry, K. (2019, June 25). 6 psychological strategies for success in life. Retrieved from https://www.verywellmind.com/how-to-be-successful-in-life-4165743

Collins, R. (2017, March 24). Top 10 ways to avoid procrastination. Retrieved from https://www.collegexpress.com/articles-and-advice/majors-and-academics/blog/top-10-ways-avoid-procrastination/

Council, Y. E. (2015, April 6). 12 ways to shift your mindset and embrace change. Retrieved from https://www.inc.com/young-entrepreneur-council/12-ways-to-shift-your-mindset-and-embrace-change.html

Gaille, B. (2017, May 19). 19 lazy procrastination statistics. Retrieved from https://brandongaille.com/17-lazy-procrastination-statistics/

Reddy, C. (2019, November 29). Top 15 reasons why passion at work is important. Retrieved from https://content.wisestep.com/passion-at-work/

Rose, J. (2019, November 13). 15 ways to invest small amounts of money (and turn it into a large amount of money). Retrieved from https://www.goodfinancialcents.com/how-to-invest-small-amounts-of-money/

Stasiulionyte, I. (2016 2). 10 tips to achieve anything you want in life. Retrieved from https://www.success.com/10-tips-to-achieve-anything-you-want-in-life/

Tracy, B. (2019, October 17). How to be successful in life [2019]: Brian Tracy. Retrieved from https://www.briantracy.com/blog/personal-success/personal-success-keys-to-success-change-your-life/